The INSIDE GUIDE

WOMEN IN U.S. HISTORY

Women in the Wild West

By Therese M. Shea

Cavendish Square

Published in 2025 by Cavendish Square Publishing, LLC
2544 Clinton Street Buffalo, NY 14224

First Edition

Website: cavendishsq.com

Library of Congress Cataloging-in-Publication Data

Names: Shea, Therese, author.
Title: Women in the Wild West / Therese M. Shea.
Description: New York : Cavendish Square Publishing, [2025] | Series: The inside guide: women in U.S. history | Includes index.
Identifiers: LCCN 2024029068 (print) | LCCN 2024029069 (ebook) | ISBN 9781502673121 (library binding) | ISBN 9781502673114 (paperback) | ISBN 9781502673138 (ebook)
Subjects: LCSH: Women pioneers–West (U.S.)–History–19th century–Juvenile literature. | Women–West (U.S.)–Juvenile literature. | West (U.S.)–Social life and customs–Juvenile literature. | Women–West (U.S.)–History–Juvenile literature. | Frontier and pioneer life–West (U.S.)–Juvenile literature.
Classification: LCC F596 .S48 2025 (print) | LCC F596 (ebook) | DDC 978–dc23/eng/20240702
LC record available at https://lccn.loc.gov/2024029068
LC ebook record available at https://lccn.loc.gov/2024029069

Editor: Therese Shea
Copyeditor: Danielle Haynes
Designer: Deanna Lepovich

The photographs in this book are used by permission and through the courtesy of: Cover Shutterstock AI Generator/Shutterstock.com; pp. 4, 7 (main), 12, 14, 16, 20 (main), 25 courtesy of the Library of Congress; p. 6 North Wind Picture Archives/Alamy Stock Photo; p. 7 (inset) 1850 Woman and Men in California Gold Rush/Wikimedia Commons; p. 8 Mary Ellen Pleasant, 1901/Wikimedia Commons; p. 10 Cattle Roundup, Great Falls, MT, Geo B Bonnell, c1890/Wikimedia Commons; p. 13 Woman on Horse, Creede, 1893/Wikimedia Commons; p. 15 Buffalo Calf Road Woman/Wikimedia Commons; p. 18 Marie Suize Pantalon (Gravure)/Wikimedia Commons; p. 19 Chinese American Woman in Traditional Dress/Wikimedia Commons; p. 20 (inset) Mary Fields/Wikimedia Commons; p. 21 (left) Cathay Williams' disability discharge document/Wikimedia Commons; p. 21 (right) RP Photo/Alamy Stock Photo; p. 22 Miss-Annie-Oakley-peerless-wingshot/Wikimedia Common; p. 24 Annie Oakley shooting over her shoulder using a hand mirror/ Wikimedia Commons; p. 26 (top) PearlHart/Wikimedia Commons; p. 26 (bottom) Belle Starr, Fort Smith, Arkansas, 1886/Wikimedia Commons; p. 29 (left) Sioux Indian travois, ca 1893 (LAROCHE 138)/Wikimedia Commons; p. 29 (right) Homesteader NE 1866/ Wikimedia Commons.

CPSIA compliance information: Batch #CWCSQ25: For further information contact Cavendish Square Publishing LLC at 1-877-980-4450.

Printed in the United States of America

CONTENTS

When people think of the Wild West, they think of cowboys, Native Americans, and gunfire. It was a time of change for the people and the land of the West.

WHERE AND WHEN

Chapter One

The Wild West wasn't just a place—it was also a time. It took place during the last half of the 19th century and encompassed a large area of land from Montana south to Texas and all the way west to the Pacific coast. It was called the "Wild" West because it had a reputation for lawlessness and violence. While movies and television have somewhat **exaggerated** that, many tales of the Wild West have some truths to them. There was more crime than in eastern U.S. states. There were also cowboys, cattle drives, gold mines, sheriffs, and outlaws.

However, the Wild West was also about people working hard to establish new lives or struggling to maintain their old lives. Many of these people were women. Women played a large role in the shaping of the American West.

Fast Fact

The Wild West is sometimes called the Old West or the American frontier.

Drawn to the West

Certain major events touched off the push west for Americans. One was the outcome of the Mexican-American War (1846–1848). It ended in the United States gaining much new territory from Mexico, including today's

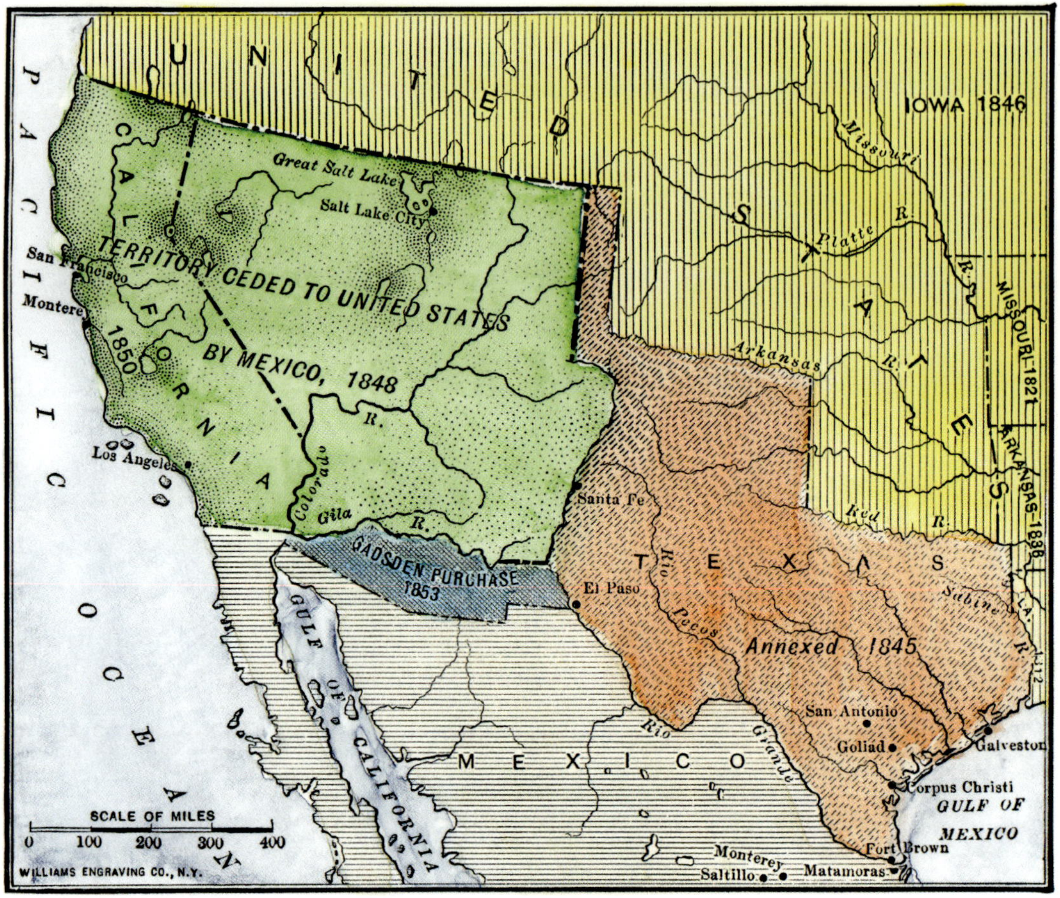

This is a map of the United States in 1850, showing the new lands acquired from Mexico after the Mexican-American War.

states of New Mexico, Utah, Nevada, California, Texas, and parts of Arizona, Colorado, Wyoming, and Kansas.

Another event that caused people to head west was the discovery of gold in California in 1848. Tens of thousands of gold seekers arrived in California in 1849 alone.

During the American Civil War (1861-1865), Congress passed the Homestead Act of 1862. It pledged 160 acres (65 hectares) of western

At first, men outnumbered women greatly during the California gold rush, but some women tried their luck at mining too.

lands to people who agreed to farm the plot. Finally, the construction of railroads and the completion of a **transcontinental** railroad in 1869 allowed for easier travel to and within the West.

Fast Fact

Miners found valuable metals in other parts of the West, too, such as the silver of the Comstock Lode near Virginia City, Nevada, discovered in 1859.

The Homestead Act of 1862 granted land claims in 30 of today's states. This photo shows the first successful claim, obtained and settled by Daniel Freeman in Nebraska.

MARY ELLEN PLEASANT

Mary Ellen Pleasant was a free Black woman who traveled from New England to San Francisco, California, in 1852. Pleasant had inherited money from her first marriage and used it to open several businesses. She employed Black workers and contributed to Black organizations. She worked as a housekeeper while she built her wealth. Pleasant sued a San Francisco **streetcar** company when a driver purposely didn't stop to pick her up. The California Supreme Court decided the case, stating that segregation, or the separation of races, on streetcars was illegal. Pleasant is sometimes called the mother of the California civil rights movement.

Mary Ellen Pleasant helped enslaved people escape to freedom in New England and may have continued to do so as a California resident.

What Women Found

The women who already lived in the West had their lives thrown into disorder with the new arrivals. Native American women faced great **upheaval**. Many struggled to establish new ways of life on **reservations**. The reservations weren't always on the historical lands of Native peoples and often weren't ideal for hunting and farming. Some Native women resisted federal orders to relocate and died in conflicts with white settlers and the U.S. military.

Many white women faced challenges establishing farms and ranches, sometimes on lands with infertile soil. Some discovered more freedoms in the West than in the East. They bought and sold property, which they couldn't do in eastern states. Some ran businesses.

Until 1865, slavery was legal in many areas, including Texas and the Utah and New Mexico territories, and even free Black Americans encountered **prejudice** in the West. Still, some Black women managed to find success in spite of the obstacles. All these experiences are part of the true history of the Wild West.

Fast Fact

Many women of Spanish or Mexican background remained on the lands given to the United States after the Mexican-American War. They had to adjust to new laws that didn't give women as many rights.

While cowboys and Native Americans sometimes had conflicts about land use, they weren't always enemies. Sometimes they traded and helped each other.

COWBOYS AND INDIANS?

Chapter Two

Many Wild West tales center on cowboys and Indians, or Native Americans. The open plains of the West were an ideal place for grazing livestock. Cowboys sometimes moved their cattle through Native American territory, which did lead to conflicts. However, a cowboy's job was to care for cattle, not fight Native Americans. Another myth? Cowboys, or cowhands as they're also called, weren't always men.

Ranch Work

While women weren't on the long cattle drives that took livestock to markets, many did the same work that male cowboys did. Women rode horses, herded livestock, and used guns. Some women owned ranches, thanks to western property laws. Susan McSween, called the cattle queen of New Mexico, owned about 5,000 cattle and became wealthy as the price of beef rose after the Civil War.

Fast Fact

Wealthy ranchers with a lot of livestock hired cowhands to work for them. People with small ranches did much of the work themselves.

Evelyn Cameron and her husband moved to Montana from

Branding was a way of marking livestock so people could identify the owner. A cowhand heated an iron with the owner's mark in a fire and then pressed it against the animal's hide.

England in the late 1880s. In her journals, she detailed her days riding horses, plowing fields, milking cows, and hunting. She did this for survival, as many women in the West did. Cameron became a talented photographer, capturing women branding and roping steer, among other skills we typically associate with cowboys.

Black women held jobs as cowhands and wranglers, or people who handle horses. Johanna "Chona" Phillips July Wilkes Lasley was a Black Seminole woman who was an excellent horse tamer in Texas. Her method of taming a horse was riding the horse into a river until it tired.

Henrietta "Aunt Rittie" Williams Foster was a cowhand in Texas. Other cowhands said she could "do anything else a man could and maybe better." Plus, she did it in long skirts while riding sidesaddle.

EVELYN'S ILLEGAL OUTFIT

After Evelyn Cameron's friend was killed when her skirt got caught in a saddle, Cameron made herself a "split skirt," which was like long, flowing pants. Her community thought this wasn't appropriate for a woman to wear. Cameron said, "Although my costume [outfit] was so full as to look like an ordinary walking dress when the wearer was on foot, it created a small sensation. So great at first was the prejudice against any divided garment in Montana that a warning was given [to] me to **abstain** from riding on the streets of Miles City lest [or else] I might be arrested!"

In the 1800s, most women wore dresses or skirts when they rode horses. In some places, they had to, by law. They usually rode sidesaddle, with both their feet on the same side of the horse.

Native Women Fight Back

Cowboys didn't cause the largest conflicts with Native Americans. White settlers—and the U.S. government— continually pushed Native groups off valuable land. When the U.S. military got involved, Native Americans often were no match. That didn't stop many, including women, from resisting.

While Native American women took care of the home and family, much like white women did, Native women often had more of a say in community decisions such as going to war and relocating.

Fast Fact

One famous Wild West clash was the Battle of the Little Bighorn in 1876. After the Sioux refused to leave the Black Hills, an army unit led by George Armstrong Custer attacked Chief Sitting Bull's village. The Sioux, Northern Cheyenne, and Arapaho outnumbered the U.S. soldiers and won the battle.

The Native American victory at the Battle of the Little Bighorn in today's Montana was short-lived. More U.S. military arrived and forced the Sioux and their allies to surrender.

Fast Fact

Geronimo was an Apache chief who spent most of his life fighting settlers and soldiers in the Southwest. He asked an Apache woman named Lozen to be his negotiator with the U.S. army.

Just days before the Battle of the Little Bighorn, Buffalo Calf Road Woman had fought against the U.S. army with Cheyenne warriors led by Lakota leader Crazy Horse. She saved her wounded brother.

Some Native women even joined in battles as warriors.

Native American women fought against U.S. troops in the Battle of the Little Bighorn in 1876. According to Cheyenne history, a Northern Cheyenne woman named Buffalo Calf Road Woman knocked Lieutenant Colonel George Armstrong Custer from his horse. She may have even killed him.

Despite the resistance from many Native men and women, the U.S. government pushed most Native Americans off their lands and onto reservations by 1900, threatening their traditional ways of life. Many lived in poverty.

An 1856 illustration shows a wagon train of settlers traveling west together.

MINERS, DRIVERS, AND MORE

Chapter Three

While many who moved west established farms or ranches, some hoped to find quicker wealth in mines. Most women arrived with their families, but some came alone, viewing the West as a new start in life. That was the case for Ellen "Captain" Jack.

Mining for Riches

Ellen Jack moved to the West after most of her family had died. She opened a **boardinghouse** in Colorado and bought a share in a nearby silver mine, which made her wealthy. Mining towns were especially dangerous places for a rich woman. Jack always had her gun ready. She shot several men who tried to do her harm or rob her, but she was never sent to jail.

While some women panned for gold or sought silver in mines, others discovered it was more profitable to provide services to miners. Women did laundry, sewed clothes, or cooked food. As mining camps turned into towns and cities,

Fast Fact

The U.S. Army found gold in the Black Hills of South Dakota in 1874. Gold mining here, in Native territory, began events that led to the Battle of the Little Bighorn.

Marie Suize moved to California from France in 1850 during the gold rush. She became a successful miner and winemaker.

Fast Fact

Marie Suize was arrested more than once for wearing pants. Her nickname, which she herself used, was Marie Pantalon. (*Pantalon* is the French word for pants.)

some women set up businesses. In many mining communities, more money was made in business than in the mines.

Drivers

Professions considered acceptable for women were limited in the 1800s, even in the West. Most were related to the work that women traditionally did in the home, such as making clothes and food or caring for people. However, some women did well at jobs that men usually held.

Charley Parkhurst had a tough reputation. Born Charlotte Parkhurst, Charley ran away from a New England orphanage at a young age and found work at a stable while dressed as a boy. Parkhurst maintained

A SAD HISTORY

Many Chinese men immigrated, or moved to, the United States during the California gold rush. A smaller number of women also made the journey. These women faced a hard life in mining towns. While some found employment in laundry, housekeeping, and seamstress businesses, others were treated as if they were enslaved. In fact, some had been sold by their families or tricked into leaving China. People forced these women to work and even kept them locked up. In 1854, California courts decided Chinese people couldn't speak for themselves during trials, opening the door for crimes against them to go unpunished.

In the 1800s, Chinese immigrants, such as the woman shown here, came to the United States because of widespread poverty in their homeland. Americans treated them poorly. In 1882, a federal law barred further Chinese people from coming to the United States. This lasted for 10 years.

A stagecoach was a large, closed vehicle pulled by horses. It was large enough to carry passengers and often mail and other goods.

this identity, learning how to handle horses and later becoming known as the best stagecoach driver in the East.

Parkhurst moved to California during the gold rush and worked for several stagecoach businesses, sometimes transporting gold. Parkhurst's stagecoach was robbed in 1858. When the same bandit tried to rob it the next year, Parkhurst shot and killed him. After Parkhurst died in 1879, friends discovered Parkhurst had been born a female.

"Stagecoach" Mary Fields was the first Black woman to deliver mail for the U.S. Post Office. Hired in 1895, Fields's star

Mary Fields became beloved in Cascade, Montana. While she had a tough personality, she was kind to children and good to her neighbors.

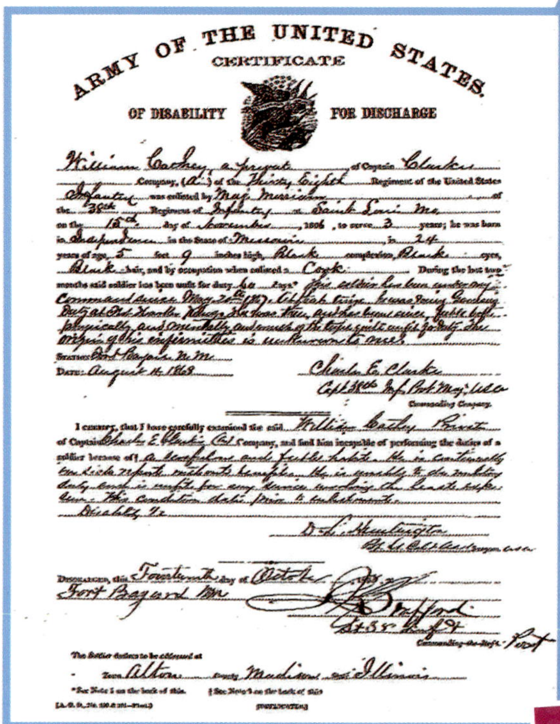
ARMY OF THE UNITED STATES.
CERTIFICATE
OF DISABILITY FOR DISCHARGE

William Cathey a private of Captain Clarke's Company, (A) of the Thirty Eighth Regiment of the United States Infantry was enlisted by Maj. Merriam of the 38th Regiment of Infantry at Saint Louis Mo. on the 15th day of November, 1866, to serve 3 years; he was born in Independence in the State of Missouri, is 24 years of age, 5 feet 9 inches high, Black complexion, Black eyes, Black hair, and by occupation when enlisted a Cook. During the last two months said soldier has been unfit for duty 60 days. [illegible]

Station: Fort Bayard N.M.
Date: August 14, 1868
Charles E. Clarke
Capt 38th Inf. [illegible]
Commanding Company.

I certify, that I have carefully examined the said William Cathey Private of Captain Charles E. Clarke's Co A Company, and find him incapable of performing the duties of a soldier because of [illegible]
Disability [illegible]

D. L. Huntington
[illegible]

Discharged, this Fourteenth day of October [illegible]
Fort Bayard N.M.
[illegible]
Commanding the Post

The Soldier desires to be addressed at
Town Alton County Madison State Illinois

* See Note 1 on the back of this. † See Note 2 on the back of this.

Cathay Williams (known as William Cathay in the army) was discharged, or released, from the army after a doctor discovered she was a woman. Her discharge papers are shown here.

route was located near Cascade, Montana. (A star route was a route with a small population, usually in a rural area.) Delivering mail in the Wild West wasn't a safe job. Fields had to deal with thieves, wolves, impassable roads, and terrible weather. She carried two guns and was said to have fought off a pack of wolves. Fields drove her route for eight years.

Fast Fact

Another woman with an unusual job, Cathay Williams disguised herself as a man to join the U.S. Army in the 1860s. She was the only woman to serve with the Buffalo Soldiers, all-Black army units in the West.

Although Annie Oakley, who's shown here, became a Wild West legend, she was born in Ohio. She rose to fame by thrilling crowds with her marksmanship.

FAMOUS AND INFAMOUS

Chapter Four

Produced by William "Buffalo Bill" Cody beginning in 1883, his Wild West traveling show included a play about the Battle of the Little Bighorn, wild animals such as bison, and cowboy skills. It wasn't completely truthful about life in the West, but crowds were fascinated. Shows such as this helped grow the myth of the Wild West. Some women played a starring role in these shows.

Putting on a Show

Annie Oakley may have sharpened her marksmanship by hunting to support her family at an early age. After winning a shooting contest as a teenager in 1875 (in which she met and defeated her future husband), she began to tour the country showing off her skills. At a tour stop in Minnesota in 1884, Oakley met Lakota Sioux chief Sitting Bull, who respected her skill

Fast Fact

Annie Oakley wanted to gather a unit of women sharpshooters like herself to fight in the Spanish-American War (1898) and World War I (1914-1918), but the U.S. government didn't accept the offers.

Annie Oakley could shoot a dime thrown into the air and shoot over her shoulder using a mirror.

and gave her the nickname "Little Sure Shot." The next year, she joined Buffalo Bill's Wild West show and toured with it for more than 15 years.

Martha "Calamity Jane" Cannary was born in Missouri in 1852 and moved to Montana as a young girl. There, she became known for her skill driving teams of horses. She moved to Deadwood, South Dakota, in 1876, during the gold rush there. According to some accounts, she was a scout for George Armstrong Custer at one time. She also may have rescued stagecoach passengers from a Native American attack. These accounts may not have been true, but they won her a place in Buffalo Bill's show in the 1890s.

Calamity Jane's life inspired many tales. The truth and the tales have become mixed. However, she was a great horse rider and sharpshooter.

Outlaws

Some women were as fierce as any male outlaws of the West. After seeing Buffalo Bill's Wild West show in 1893, Pearl Hart left her family in Canada to seek out a new life in Arizona. There, she pulled off several robberies before

Fast Fact

At her 1899 trial, outlaw Pearl Hart said, "I shall not be tried under a law in which my sex had no voice in making." She was acquitted but later sent to jail for other crimes.

Pearl Hart may have turned to a life of crime to help pay for her mother's medical bills.

police captured her. The newspapers called her the "bandit queen."

Myra "Belle" Starr was another outlaw celebrity. Born in Missouri around 1848, she moved to Texas after her town of Carthage burned in the Civil War and later to the Oklahoma Territory. Belle and her husband helped hide outlaws on their ranch, including Jesse James. Belle was involved in horse stealing and was accused of robbing a post office while dressed as a man.

Belle Starr was shot in the back in 1889. Her murder was never solved.

WOMEN'S SUFFRAGE

Women's rights supporters found allies in western state and territorial legislatures. Their first success was in the Wyoming territory, which gave women suffrage, or the right to vote, in 1869. Utah's legislature gave women the right to vote the following year. Congress stripped it away in 1887 in a bid to end **polygamy** in Utah's Mormon Church. When Wyoming became a state in 1890 and Utah in 1896, their constitutions granted women suffrage. (Native American and Black women were often blocked from voting, however.) These successes helped gain support for national suffrage, guaranteed in the 19th Amendment to the U.S. Constitution, which became law in 1920.

Fast Fact

In 1890, the U.S. Census Bureau stated that the American frontier was closed. This meant that there were no longer large areas of unsettled land.

The End of the Era

By 1900, many states had formed from western territories. Governments and law-enforcing agencies were established. Towns and cities continued to grow. The U.S. government had forced Native Americans to largely remain on reservations. The era of the Wild West was over.

The West had given some women opportunities they couldn't find in the East. Some found success, others disappointment. Certainly, the United States was forever altered by the movement westward, and women played a key role in that change.

A TIMELINE OF FAMOUS WILD WEST WOMEN

1850
Marie Suize arrives in California to mine gold during the gold rush.

1858
Charley Parkhurst shoots and kills a stagecoach bandit.

1862
The Homestead Act is passed, granting western lands to U.S. men and women.

1866
Mary Ellen Pleasant sues a San Francisco streetcar company.

1870
Louisa Swain of Wyoming is the first woman to legally cast a vote in a general election.

1876
Buffalo Calf Road Woman fights in the Battle of the Little Bighorn.
Calamity Jane arrives in Deadwood, South Dakota, during a gold rush.

1885
Annie Oakley joins Buffalo Bill's Wild West show as a sharpshooter.

1886
Lozen, an Apache woman who worked as a negotiator, is imprisoned after Geronimo surrenders to the U.S. Army.

1889
Belle Starr is shot in the back while on horseback.

1895
Mary Fields is hired to carry mail on a U.S. mail route.

1899
Pearl Hart stands trial for robbing a stagecoach.

THINK ABOUT IT!

1. Why do you think women in some western areas were allowed freedoms such as owning property, but not others, such as wearing pants?
2. Why do you think Americans viewed Chinese immigrants with suspicion? How could this prejudice have been overcome?
3. Why do you think Buffalo Bill's Wild West show was such a hit with audiences around the world?
4. Why do you think western states were the first to give women the right to vote?

GLOSSARY

abstain: To make a choice not to do something.

acquit: To declare that someone is not guilty of a crime.

ally: One of two or more people or groups who work together.

boardinghouse: A place where people pay to live and have meals.

exaggerate: To think of or describe something as larger or greater than it really is.

marksmanship: Skill in shooting.

negotiator: One who tries to come to an agreement with someone else.

polygamy: The practice of having more than one wife or husband at one time.

prejudice: Unfair treatment of someone because of their race, sex, religious beliefs, or some other feature.

reservation: Land set aside by the U.S. government for Native Americans to live on.

streetcar: A vehicle that runs on track laid in the streets.

transcontinental: Extending across a continent.

upheaval: A big change that causes confusion, anger, or other bad emotions.

FIND OUT MORE

Books

Bearce, Stephanie. *Awesome, Disgusting, Unusual Facts About the Wild West*. Mankato, MN: Black Rabbit Books, 2024.

Bell, Samantha. *The "Wild" West*. Ann Arbor, MI: Cherry Lake Press, 2024.

Connors, Kathleen. *Forgotten Facts About Life in the Wild West*. Buffalo, NY: Enslow Publishing, 2024.

Websites

PBS: Women of the Wild West
www.pbs.org/opb/historydetectives/feature/women-of-the-wild-west/
Read more about some of the famous gun-toting women of the West.

7 Famous Native American Women with Remarkable Stories
www.oldwest.org/famous-native-american-women/
Learn more about several notable Native American women.

Wonderopolis: When Did the American Old West End?
wonderopolis.org/wonder/when-did-the-american-old-west-end
Check out this overview of how the West changed.

INDEX